This Password Book Belongs To

REMEMBER: Keep This Book Safe!

Dedication

This Password Keeper Log Book is dedicated to all the people out there who want to record their passwords and document their findings in the process.

You are my inspiration for producing books and I'm honored to be a part of keeping all of your password notes and records organized.

This journal notebook will help you record the details of your online internet passwords.

Thoughtfully put together with these sections to record: Website, Username, Password, and Notes.

How to Use this Book

The purpose of this book is to keep all of your password and username notes all in one place. It will help keep you organized.

This Password Keeper Log Book will allow you to accurately document every detail about your internet passwords.

Here are examples of the prompts for you to fill in and write about your experience in this book:

1. Website - Write the name of the websites.
2. Username - Record your usernames.
3. Password - Log your online passwords.
4. Notes - A place to record any additional information you want.

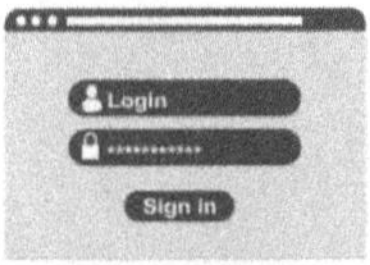

Website	Username	Password

Notes

Website	Username	Password

Notes

Website	Username	Password

Notes

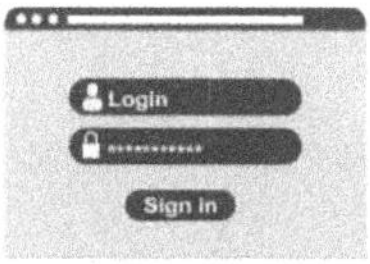

Website	Username	Password

Notes

Website	Username	Password

Notes

Website	Username	Password

Notes

Website	Username	Password

Notes

Website	Username	Password

Notes

Website	Username	Password

Notes

Website	Username	Password

Notes

Website	Username	Password

Notes

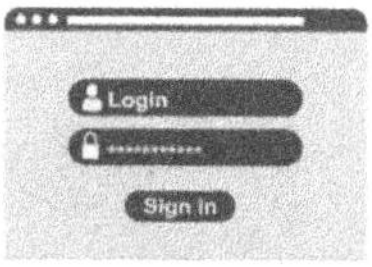

Website	Username	Password

Notes

Website	Username	Password

Notes

Website	Username	Password

Notes

Website	Username	Password

Notes

Website	Username	Password

Notes

Website	Username	Password

Notes

Website	Username	Password

Notes

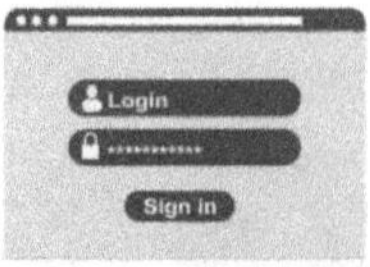

Website	Username	Password

Notes

Website	Username	Password

Notes

Website	Username	Password

Notes

Website	Username	Password

Notes

Website	Username	Password

Notes

Website	Username	Password

Notes

Website	Username	Password

Notes

Website	Username	Password

Notes

Website	Username	Password

Notes

Website	Username	Password

Notes

Website	Username	Password

Notes

Website	Username	Password

Notes

Website	Username	Password

Notes

Website	Username	Password

Notes

Website	Username	Password

Notes

Website	Username	Password

Notes

Website	Username	Password

Notes

Website	Username	Password

Notes

Website	Username	Password

Notes

Website	Username	Password

Notes

Website	Username	Password

Notes

Website	Username	Password

Notes

Website	Username	Password

Notes

Website	Username	Password

Notes

Website	Username	Password

Notes

Website	Username	Password

Notes

Website	Username	Password

Notes

Website	Username	Password

Notes

Website	Username	Password

Notes

Website	Username	Password

Notes

Website	Username	Password

Notes

Website	Username	Password

Notes

Website	Username	Password

Notes

Website	Username	Password

Notes

Website	Username	Password

Notes

Website	Username	Password

Notes

Website	Username	Password

Notes

Website	Username	Password

Notes

Website	Username	Password

Notes

Website	Username	Password

Notes

Website	Username	Password

Notes

Website	Username	Password

Notes

Website	Username	Password

Notes

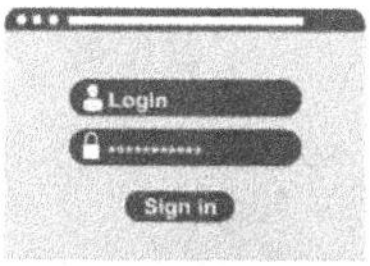

Website	Username	Password

Notes

Website	Username	Password

Notes

Website	Username	Password

Notes

Website	Username	Password

Notes

Website	Username	Password

Notes

Website	Username	Password

Notes

Website	Username	Password

Notes

Website	Username	Password

Notes

Website	Username	Password

Notes

Website	Username	Password

Notes

Website	Username	Password

Notes

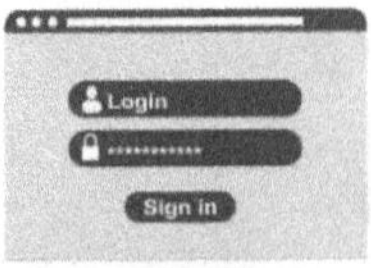

Website	Username	Password

Notes

Website	Username	Password

Notes

Website	Username	Password

Notes

Website	Username	Password

Notes

Website	Username	Password

Notes

Website	Username	Password

Notes

Website	Username	Password

Notes

Website	Username	Password

Notes

Website	Username	Password

Notes

Website	Username	Password

Notes

Website	Username	Password

Notes

Website	Username	Password

Notes

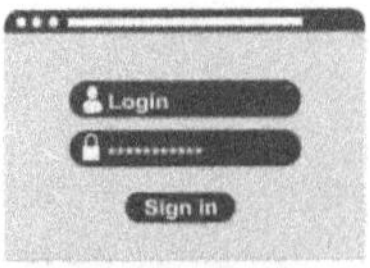

Website	Username	Password

Notes

Website	Username	Password

Notes

Website	Username	Password

Notes

Website	Username	Password

Notes

Website	Username	Password

Notes

Website	Username	Password

Notes

Website	Username	Password

Notes

Website	Username	Password

Notes

Website	Username	Password

Notes

Website	Username	Password

Notes

Website	Username	Password

Notes

Website	Username	Password

Notes

Website	Username	Password

Notes

Website	Username	Password

Notes

Website	Username	Password

Notes

Website	Username	Password

Notes

Website	Username	Password

Notes

www.ingramcontent.com/pod-product-compliance
Lightning Source LLC
Chambersburg PA
CBHW071300050326
40690CB00011B/2477